ANIMAL
PUZZLES & GAMES

Matthew Rossetti

L HAMMOND World Atlas
Part of the Langenscheidt Publishing Group

Photo and Illustration Credits:

The following images provided by Shutterstock.com

(page 3) Eric Isselée **(4)** James DeBoer (turtle) • Andrejs Jegorovs (elephant) • Steffen Foerster Photography (elephant seal) • Eric Isselée (fox) **(5)** Eric Isselée (puppy, kitten, duckling, calf, cub) • xjrshimada (bunny) • clearviewstock (lamb) • Keith Tarrier (seal pup) • Werg (larva) • Tap10 (kangaroo) • **(6)** Eric Isselée (pig, ferret) • Matt Antonino (frog) • Jill Lang (parrot) • fivespots (spider) **(7)** Andrey Ushakov (flamingo) **(8)** Andrey Ushakov (parrot) •Jeff R. Clow (armadillo)• Joshua Lewis (rabbit) • Christian Musat (gorilla) • zimmytws (shark) • Oleg Kozlov, Sophy Kozlova (tiger) • Anyka (bee) • Antonio V. Oquias (pig) • DMK (croc) • bernd.neeser (caterpillar) **(10)** javarman (bat) • MARKABOND (dolphin) • Regien Paassen (panda) • Eric Isselée (dog) • Rusty Dodson (zebra) • Jong Kiam Soon (chimp)• Emilia Stasiak (mouse) **(11)** Eric Isselée **(12)** Edwin Verin **(14)** Eric Isselée (chameleon, alligator, tortoise, dragon) • fivespots (gecko, snake) • Norma Cornes (komodo) **(16)** Eric Isselée (corn snake, king snake) • fivespots (boa) • iconex (cobra) **(18)** Jamie Wilson (bg) • Michelle D. Milliman (toad) • Bruce MacQueen (salamander) **(19)** alle (frog) **(20)** Borislav Gnjidic (bg) • Bruce MacQueen (cardinal) • FloridaStock (eagle) • nialat (eagle head) **(21)** Al Mueller (hummingbird) **(22)** PhotoBarmaley (bg) • Gregg Williams (robin) **(23)** Hannu Liivaar (macaw) • Gregg Williams (blue jay) • Stephen Mcsweeny (hawk) • 5464316719 (peacock) • Manuel Blanco (pelican) **(24)** Ravi (bg) • Robertas (bugs) • Joanna Zopoth-Lipiejko (caterpillar) **(25)** Ravi (bg) • Raymond Kasprzak (fly) • Vladimir Vitek (beetle) • fivespots (spider) • Evgeniy Ayupov (mantis)• Els Jooren (ladybug) • Mau Horng (grasshopper) • Sven Hoppe (wasp) • Eric Isselée (dragonfly) • PetrP (cricket) • Sharon Day (firefly) • Vinicius Tupinamba (centipede) • Dole (butterfly) • Potapov Alexander (ant) • vnlit (bee) **(28)** Kaminskiy (bg) • EcoPrint (crab) • David Pruter (orca) • Tatjana Rittner (fish) • Alex James Bramwell (turtle) • Raymond Connetta (puffer) **(29)** Ian Scott **(30)** Kaminskiy (bg) • Yai (crab) • Nina Malyna (starfish) • Stephen Aaron Rees (urchin) • Ovidiu Iordachi (dolphins) • Joy Brown (jellyfish) • Kurilin Gennadiy Nikolaevich (shark) **(32)** Zavodskov Anatoliy Nikolaevich (bg) • Eric Isselée (animals) • Leonid Anna Dedukh (cow head) **(33)** Selena (chicken) **(34)** Jiri (bg) • Eric Isselée (animals) **(35)** Sascha Burkard (guinea pig, frog) • Tony Campbell (turtle) • fivespots (snake) • Johanna Goodyear (fish) • Eric Isselée (hamster, parrot, rabbit) • Mityukhin Oleg Petrovich (lizard) **(36)** Pakhnyushcha (bg) • Eric Isselée (rabbit, fox, deer, raccoon) • Jaren Jai Wicklund (chipmunk) • Konstantins Visnevskis (mouse) • Bruce MacQueen (woodpecker) • stocknadia (squirrel) **(38)** Hydromet (bg) • John Bell (snake) **(39)** Francesco Abrignani (jack) • Eric Isselée (raven) • Ritu Manoj Jethani (iguana) • Jill Lang (hawk) • Dvoretskiy Igor Vladimirovich (camel) • jocicalek (scorpion) **(40)** mypokcik (bg) • Pichugin Dmitry (lovebirds) • Sascha Burkard (frog) • Harley Couper (toucan) • Xavier Marchant (orangutan) Alexander Yu Zotov (capybara) **(41)** Morgan Lane Photography (monkey) • Holger W. (butterfly) • Nikola I (silhouettes) **(42)** faberfoto (bg) • Nikola I (elephant) • Paul Merrett (giraffe) • Brad Thompson (giraffe head) **(43)** R. Gino Santa Maria (meerkats) • Eric Isselée (jackal) **(44)** Kirsty Pargeter (bg) • Vladimir Melnik (seal) • Anna Dzondnza (owl) • Steve Estvanik (penguin) • Serg Zastavkin (wolverine) • Alasdair Turner Photography (ptarmigan) • Tom Curtis (tern) • Ronnie Howard (ermine) • Vasilily Koval (musk ox) • Susan Flashman (penguin 1) • Zebra0209 (penguin 2) • Jan Martin Will (penguin 3) **(45)** Lena Lir (mom) • Ekaterina Starshaya (baby) **(46)** Suto Norbert Zsolt (bg) • Eric Isselée (kangaroo, cockatoo, galah), Julien Grondin (crocodile) • Patsy A. Jacks (Tasmanian devil) **(47)** Eric Isselée (monitor) **(48)** Serghei Starus (bg) Top: Adrov Andriy (frog) • Ultrashock (skunk) • Carolina K. Smith, M.D. (moth) • Ewan Chesser (tarsier) • Vasiliy Koval (owl) • Bottom: Ultrashock (skunk) • Maxim Tupikov (moth) • Eric Isselée (raccoon) • teekaygee (opossum) • dirkr (owl) • Raid Khalil (bat) • Daria (mouse) • Vadim Volodin (hedgehog) • dmitriyd (catfish) • Arie v.d.Wolde (frog) • Kurt_G (cricket) **(52)** fivespots (frog)

Additional backgrounds and illustrations by Matt Rossetti

Crossword puzzles and some word search puzzles generated by www.puzzle-maker.com

Copyright ©2009 Hammond World Atlas Corporation

Published in the United States and its territories and Canada by
HAMMOND WORLD ATLAS CORPORATION
Part of the Langenscheidt Publishing Group
36-36 33rd Street
Long Island City, NY 11106

Cover design: Jeff Beebe

Cover credits: Front and back cover images from iStockphoto.com, Shutterstock.com, Photos.com, and 123RF.com

Printed and bound in Canada

ISBN-13: 978-0841-610910

Table of Contents

Animals-A-Go-Go!

CREATURE COMBOS

Pair up the name of an animal from group A with one from group B to make a completely different animal. Write the names of your combo animals in the spaces provided. The first one is done for you.

Group A:

ant
bull
cat
chicken
deer
~~elephant~~
horse
kangaroo
fox
stag
tiger
wolf

1) ELEPHANT SEAL

2) _____

3) _____

4) _____

5) _____

6) _____

7) _____

8) _____

9) _____

10) _____

11) _____

12) _____

Group B:

beetle
fish
fly
frog
hawk
hound
lion
rat
~~seal~~
shark
spider
tick

FUN FACT:
The elephant seal, named for its large nose, can dive for periods of up to 2 hours without coming up for air.

BEASTLY BABIES

Baby animals often go by specific names according to their species (for example, a baby whale is called a **calf**). Use the list of animal mothers below to fill in the puzzle with the names of their young.

Across:
4) bear
8) butterfly
9) cockroach
10) dog
12) cat
14) kangaroo
16) goose
17) cow
19) chicken
21) eagle
23) gorilla
25) fish
26) deer
27) pigeon

Down:
1) duck
2) turtle
3) spider
5) rabbit
6) sheep
7) frog
11) seal
13) pig
15) owl
18) skunk
20) goat
22) beetle
24) horse

TALK LIKE THE ANIMALS

Look at the list of animals below. See if you can find and circle the **sound** that each one makes. Look across, up, down, diagonally, and backwards.

BEE   GOOSE
BIRD   HORSE
CAT   LION
CHICKEN   MOUSE
COW   OWL
CROW   PARROT
DOG   PIG
DONKEY   SHEEP
DUCK   SNAKE
FROG   TURKEY

M	E	O	W	A	H	E	E	H
C	O	G	N	E	I	G	H	O
H	O	O	T	S	C	A	W	N
I	H	B	C	Q	U	A	C	K
R	I	B	A	U	R	O	A	R
P	S	L	O	A	C	Z	K	A
A	S	E	D	W	O	Z	K	B
C	L	U	C	K	O	U	N	D
L	E	D	R	I	B	B	I	T
S	Q	U	E	A	K	O	O	O

After you're done, read the leftover letters from left to right to find the **Secret Sound!** Can you guess what animal makes this sound?

_____

ANIMAL SCRAMBLE

Unscramble each of these animal names and write your answers in the numbered rows that go across. When you're done, read the blue column of letters from top to bottom to discover what all of these animals have in common.

1) TOPYNH
2) TEFRRE
3) ERGIT
4) LICOCREDO
5) KRASH
6) YECOOT
7) CONFAL
8) DRIPES
9) SOOPTUC

AMAZING ARMOR

The pangolin is an anteater with a thick, armored coat. See if you can make your way through his maze of scales.

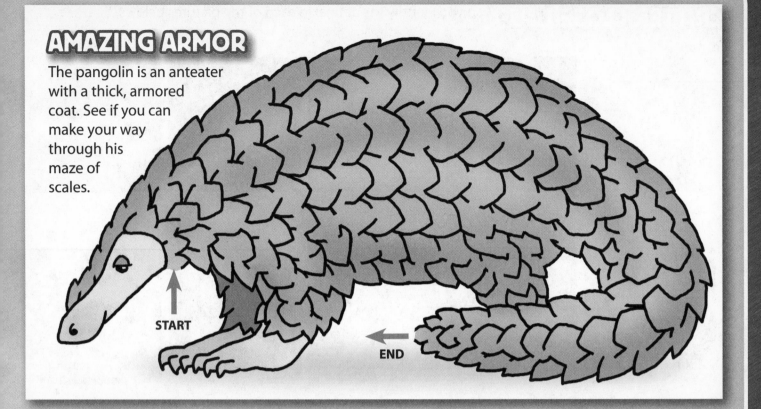

START

END

GROUP TROOP

When a group of the same type of animal are together, they're often given a special group name (for example, a **flock** of sheep). Using words from the list at the bottom, fill in the group names for the animals below.

1) A _____ of fish

2) A _____ of beavers

3) A _____ of hyenas

4) A _____ of elephants

5) A _____ of flamingos

6) A _____ of wolves

7) A _____ of lions

8) A _____ of bees

9) A _____ of geese

10) A _____ of clams

11) A _____ of bats

12) A _____ of crows

bed	family	murder	school
cackle	gaggle	pack	stand
cloud	herd	pride	swarm

CRITTER CLOSE-UPS
Can you identify the animal in each of the pictures below?

1) _____ 2) _____ 3) _____ 4) _____ 5) _____

6) _____ 7) _____ 8) _____ 9) _____ 10) _____

SIMILE SAFARI
Animals are used in many well-known sayings. See if you can complete these phrases using the list of animals provided.

1) Blind as a _____   7) Quiet as a _____

2) Sly as a _____   8) Strong as an _____

3) Sick as a _____   9) Slippery as an _____

4) Gentle as a _____   10) Happy as a _____

5) Stubborn as a _____   11) Free as a _____

6) Busy as a _____   12) Proud as a _____

bat	clam	fox	mule
bee	dog	lamb	ox
bird	eel	mouse	peacock

A SILLY STORY

Here's something fun to do with a friend. Without showing him or her the story below, ask for a word for each blank space based on the description below the line. When finished, read their silly story back to them!

World-famous zoologist _____ has just made a startling new
                        name of someone you know

discovery; A(n) _____ known as the _____! The _____ is
              animal type (mammal,   silly word   same silly word
              insect, reptile, etc.)

a most unusual animal that looks like a cross between a(n) _____ and
                                                          animal

a(n) _____. It has _____ skin with _____ stripes on its
        noun   color   color

_____. It's _____ is shaped like a(n) _____, which it
  body part   body part   noun

wiggles when it is _____. When fully grown, a(n) _____ will be about
                    emotion   same silly word

_____ feet tall and weigh well over _____ pounds. Its diet consists
  number   number

mainly of _____, but it has been known to eat _____ or even a(n)
            food   food

_____ if really hungry.
  noun

This animal is native to _____, but a variant known as the_____
                          country   adjective

_____ has been spotted in the _____ of _____. When
same silly word   place (plural)   country

threatened, it lets out a cry of " _____" as a warning not to get too close.
                                   funny sound

If you happen to hear this cry, never fear; just pretend to be a _____ and soon the
                                                                  noun

beast will lose interest and go about its business.

Mammal Mania!

See if you can find the names of 45 mammals hidden in the puzzle below.
Look across, up, down, diagonally, and backwards.

antelope
armadillo
badger
bat
bear
beaver
camel
cat
cow
coyote
deer
dog
dolphin
elephant
ferret
fox
giraffe
goat
gopher
gorilla
horse
hyena
lemur

lion
llama
marten
mink
monkey
moose
mouse
otter
panda
pig
raccoon
rat
rhinoceros
seal
skunk
squirrel
tiger
walrus
whale
wolf
yak
zebra

```
B A D G E R H I N O C E R O S
E T T O E S U O M H F L O W Q
A E P O L E T N A E M E Y O U
R R C N S P S N R A T P T C I
E R G O E E H O T R Y H I M R
H E A O Y M A I E M A A A G R
P F H C A O L L N R R N S I E
O S O C T T T R B M H T K W L
G I R A F F E E A O O K U H E
O D S R R G Z D T O W N N A A
R O E E I L I A H S A I K L N
I G E T I L C A M E L M Y E E
L D A T L A D N A P R P A F Y
L B P O O M P L E M U R K O H
A O T B E A V E R A S M U X S
```

After you're done, read the leftover letters from left to right
to find the name of the **Mystery Mammal!**

_____

10

BIG KITTY CROSSWORD

Can you fit the names of these big cats into the puzzle grid? The words can go across and down. There's a small C-A-T to help you get started.

CHEETAH
COUGAR
JAGUAR
LEOPARD
LION
LYNX
OCELOT
TIGER

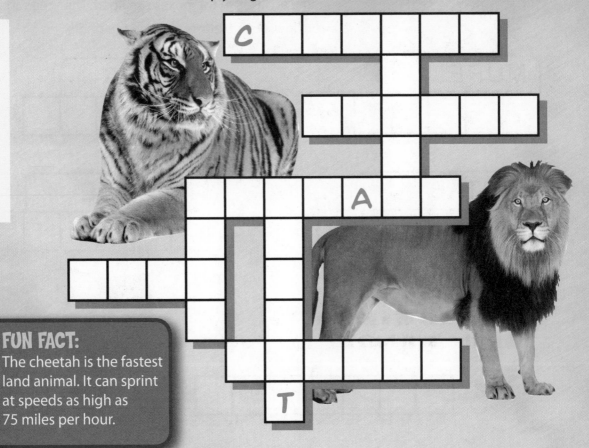

FUN FACT:
The cheetah is the fastest land animal. It can sprint at speeds as high as 75 miles per hour.

A PRICKLY PATH

How do you pet a porcupine? *Very carefully!* See if you can get through the maze below without getting "stuck".

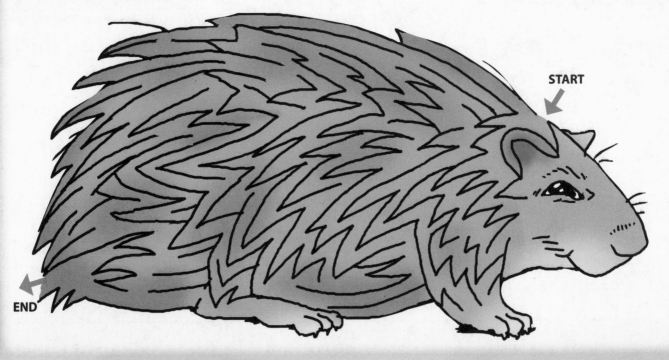

START

END

MAMMAL SCRAMBLE

Unscramble the names of the four mammals below, writing the answers in the boxes provided. Then rearrange the yellow-boxed letters to solve the riddle.

MUREL

THLOS

BIRTAB

NYODKE

Q: Which side of a gorilla has the most hair?

A: THE

PICTURE THIS

Can you name the mammals spelled out in these rebuses?

1)

2)

3)

4)

_____

_____

_____

_____

MOUSETRAP

You need a friend to play this game. Each player takes a turn connecting 2 neighboring dots with a straight line. You can go up and down and side to side, but not diagonally. Try to be the player who makes a box by adding the last line of a square. When you do, write your initial in the box and take an extra turn. Each plain square is worth 1 point; a square with a mouse in it is worth 2 points. The player with the highest score wins!

Game 1   Score_____   _____

Game 2   Score_____   _____

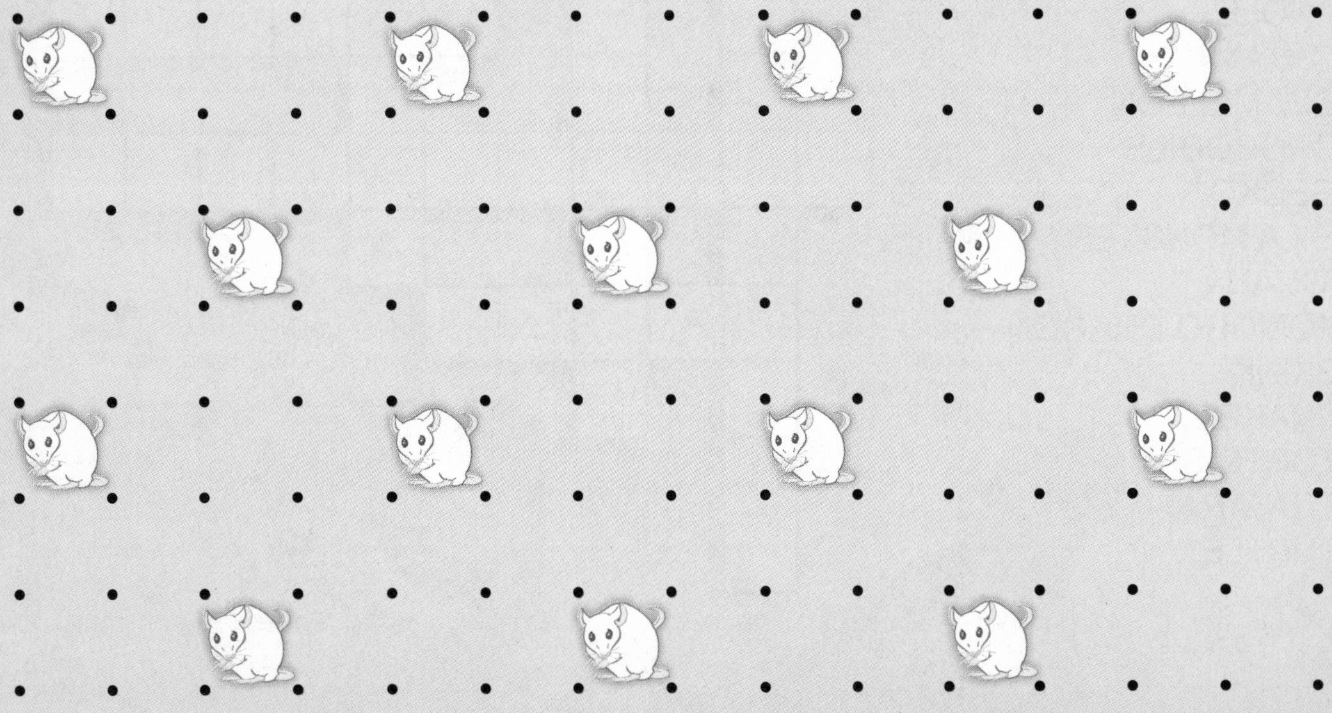

Reptile Roundup

Can you fit the names of the reptiles listed below into the puzzle grid? The words can go across and down. The reptiles left behind some of their S-C-A-L-E-S to help you get started.

ALLIGATOR
ANOLE
CAIMAN
CHAMELEON
CROCODILE
GECKO
GILA MONSTER
IGUANA
KOMODO DRAGON
SKINK
SNAKE
TORTOISE
TUATARA
TURTLE

FUN FACT:
The Komodo Dragon is the largest living species of lizard. It can reach lengths of nearly 10 feet and weigh about 150 lbs.

TURTLE TREK

Help the sea turtle hatchlings make it to the ocean. Watch out for crabs and seagulls!

SERPENT SEARCH

See if you can find the names of 35 different kinds of snakes hidden in the puzzle below. Look across, up, down, diagonally, and backwards. Words in parentheses ( ) are not hidden in the puzzle.

adder
anaconda
asp
boa constrictor
boomslang
brown (snake)
bushmaster
cobra
copperhead
coral (snake)
cottonmouth
garter (snake)
green (snake)
hognose
indigo (snake)
king (snake)
krait
mamba
mangrove (snake)
milk (snake)
mud (snake)
pipe (snake)
pit viper
rat (snake)
rattlesnake
sand (snake)
sea (snake)
sidewinder
taipan
thread (snake)
tree (snake)
vine (snake)
water moccasin
whip (snake)
wormsnake

```
A D N O C A N A R B O C B
S B O O M S L A N G T U O
P I T V I P E R H E S F A
C C E I N D I G O H I A C
H O G N O S E W M U D R O
O P T E F S G A R T E R N
S P I T N A S T K A W M S
K E S P O T E E P I I A T
K R A S E N I R I P N N R
L H N R S C M M H A D G I
I E D A L B R O W N E R C
M A M B A L E C U D R O T
A D O L A R O C P T H V O
D A E R H T I A D I H E R
D I O W O R M S N A K E A
E P G R E E N I H R O B T
R A T T L E S N A K E I A
```

After you're done, read the leftover letters from left to right to learn what word means **"a fear of snakes."**

_____

16

A SLITHERY SAYING

In North America, the venomous coral snake looks nearly identical to the nonvenomous scarlet king snake. Fortunately, there's a rhyme to help you tell the difference between the two. Starting at the snake's head, first read all of the red-banded letters. Then starting with the tail, go backward and read all of the black-banded letters to learn the rhyme.

__ __ __ __ __ __ __ __ __ __ __ __ __ __ __

__ __ __ __ , __ __ __ __ __ __ __ __ ;

__ __ __ __ __ __ __ __ __ __ __

__ __ __ __ __ __ __ __ __

Based on the rhyme, is the snake above venomous?

WHO'S HIDING ?

Shade in all of the dotted shapes in the puzzle below to see a reptilian master of disguise!

Amazing Amphibians

How many words can you make out of

SALAMANDER ?

Hint: Words can be just 1 letter and plurals count as separate words.

1) _____   17) _____   30) _____   43) _____

2) _____   18) _____   31) _____   44) _____

3) _____   19) _____   32) _____   45) _____

4) _____   20) _____   33) _____   46) _____

5) _____   21) _____   34) _____   47) _____

6) _____   22) _____   35) _____   48) _____

7) _____   23) _____   36) _____   49) _____

8) _____   24) _____   37) _____   50) _____

9) _____   25) _____   38) _____   51) _____

10) _____   26) _____   39) _____   52) _____

11) _____   27) _____   40) _____   53) _____

12) _____   28) _____   41) _____   54) _____

13) _____   29) _____   42) _____   55) _____

14) _____

15) _____

16) _____

FROGS & TOADS

Help the frogs and toads work together to get through the maze below. You must follow an alternating path of frog, toad, frog, toad all the way from start to finish. You can move up and down and side to side, but not diagonally. Don't hop on any alligators, or you just might *croak!*

START

FINISH

A NUMBER OF NEWTS

Can you find the 2 red-spotted newts that look exactly alike?

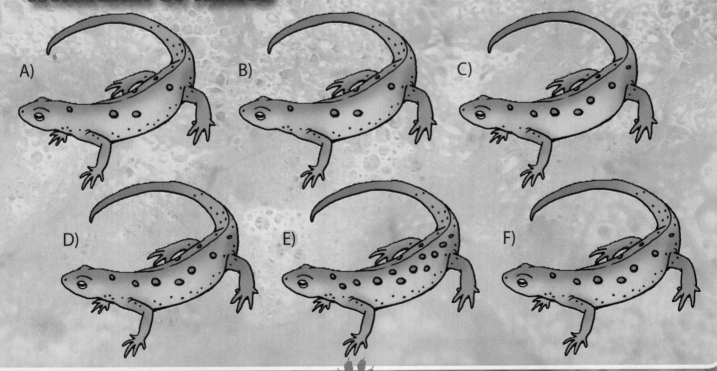

A)

B)

C)

D)

E)

F)

Bird Bonanza!

SKY-HIGH SUDOKU

Try to complete these puzzles by filling in the missing numbers. Each small empty box can be filled with a number from 1 to 9. However, each number can only be used once in each 3 x 3 grid. Also, each number can only be used once in each row across and down throughout the full puzzle.

Here is an example of what a finished puzzle looks like:

5	6	2	7	3	1	8	9	4
9	1	7	8	4	2	6	3	5
4	3	8	9	6	5	7	1	2
2	9	4	6	8	3	1	5	7
7	5	6	2	1	4	3	8	9
1	8	3	5	9	7	4	2	6
8	2	1	4	7	9	5	6	3
3	7	5	1	2	6	9	4	8
6	4	9	3	5	8	2	7	1

Puzzle 1:

	2	8	9				7	
7			5		2	8	4	6
6				8				5
3				8	2			7
2		6	3				8	
	8	7	6					
	7			6	4	5	9	
		5	2	3				
8		3			5	4		

Puzzle 2:

		7	2	6	3	8		
	2	5			8	9	4	7
	3	8		9				
5	6			4	7	8	2	
	8		2	5	3		1	6
			6			5	3	4
	9					4	5	
		2				6		3
	7	6	5			2		

FUN FACT:
The bald eagle isn't actually bald. The feathers on its head turn from brown to white at about 4 or 5 years of age.

HUMMINGBIRD HUMOR

Figure out the bird-related clues below, writing your answers in the spaces provided. Then use the numbered letters to fill in the puzzle grid and find the answer to the riddle!

A) Another name for goose feathers

26	18	19	

E) Canary color

11	7			13	23

B) Red-breasted bird

25		1		17

F) Quacking bird

12	5		16

C) What hummingbirds drink

14		3	8	4

G) Where a bird lays its eggs

	22	27	20

D) Question an owl might ask

	21	24

H) A bird's body is covered with these

	2		15	9	10		6

HMMM...

Why do hummingbirds hum?

1	2	3	4	5	6	7		8	9	10	11		12	13	14		15
	16	17	18	19		20	21	22		23	24	25	26	27			

A PAIR OF LOVEBIRDS

Can you spot 2 lovebirds that look exactly alike?

A)

B)

C)

D)

E)

F)

21

FEATHERED FUGITIVES

These birds have flown the coop! Can you get them back into their proper cages? Part of each bird's name is labeled on it's cage (for example, WOO RUS would be **Wood** Th**rus**h). Use the list of bird names on the left to help you out, but be warned—not all of them are used.

Pigmy Nuthatch
Wood Thrush
Red-breasted Nuthatch
Yellow Warbler
Mountain Chickadee
Barn Swallow
Mourning Dove
American Robin
Turtle Dove
Tree Swallow
Eastern Bluebird
Mourning Warbler

U R N
O V E

1) _____

I G M
T H A

2) _____

E R I
O B I

3) _____

L L O
R B L

4) _____

 A R N
W A L

5) _____

N T A
C K A

6) _____

PICTURE THIS

Can you name the birds spelled out in these rebuses?

1)
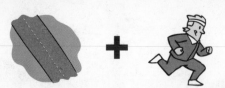

_____

2)

_____

3)

_____

4)

_____

BIRD SEARCH

See if you can find the names of 40 birds hidden in the puzzle below.
Look across, up, down, diagonally, and backwards.

```
O P A R R O T H S U R H T V H
N W B Y A N A C I L E P E U L
O L L P V K F I N C H O M L H
C W L B E L K R A L R M I T A
L R U I N A E T D E I A S U W
A E G R E T C S L N U L N R K
F L A M I N G O G Q O B S E W
C B E E K E I B C O W A S L O
A R S E G R I C N K O T G G L
R A R D O R G U H R R R R A L
D W O O D P E C K E R O E E A
I R D V D U C K L B A S B P W
N E N E A G O O S E P S E I S
A N O P I G E O N R S S W A N
L P C A N A R Y A J E U L B S
```

albatross	egret	loon	robin
blue jay	falcon	oriole	seagull
canary	finch	ostrich	sparrow
cardinal	flamingo	owl	swallow
condor	goose	parrot	swan
crane	grebe	peacock	thrush
cuckoo	hawk	pelican	vulture
dove	hummingbird	pigeon	warbler
duck	kestrel	quail	woodpecker
eagle	lark	raven	wren

Can you find 3 bugs below that *don't* match any others?

CREEPY CRAWLY CROSSWORD

Use the clues to fill in the puzzle and test your knowledge about all things insect-like!

Across:

1) an adult maggot

3) chirps by rubbing its legs together

5) insect with a shell

7) tiny bugs that swarm at dusk

8) makes honey

9) a tiny, flying bloodsucker

11) looks like it's saying "grace"

13) a yellowjacket is not a bee, but a _____

15) where 8 across calls home

16) its name means "100 feet"

19) named after a fire-breather

20) lights up to attract a mate

21) egg-laying ant or bee

Down:

1) makes a dog itch

2) lawn leaper

4) common household pest

6) eats wood

8) tastes with its feet

10) 8-legged arachnid

12) flying bug that's attracted to light at night

14) will ruin your picnic

17) red-spotted beetle

18) blood-sucking parasite

BUZZZZZZZ...

Help this bee get through the honeycomb!

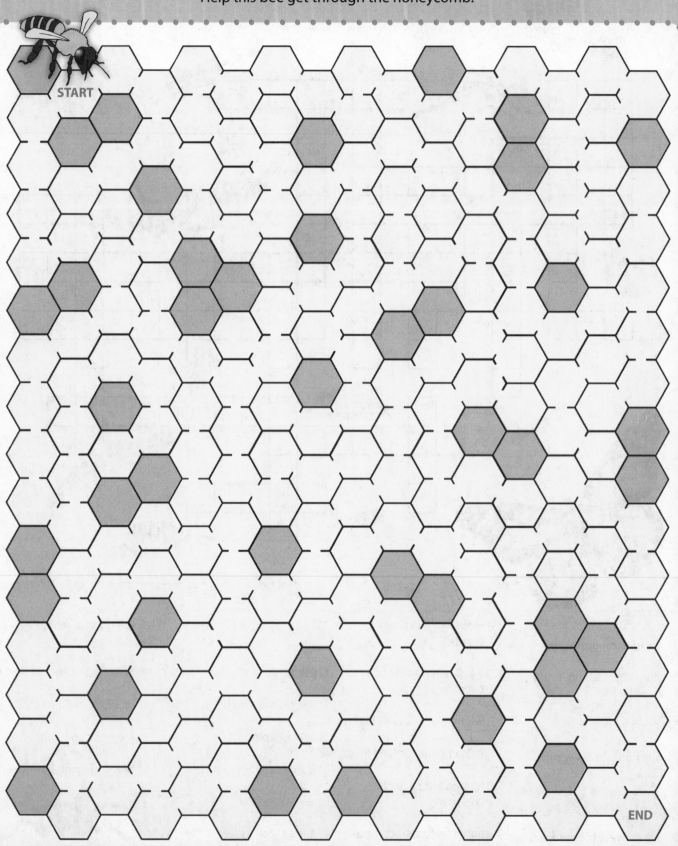

START

END

DOT-TO-DOT

Connect the dots from 1 to 45 to see who's there!

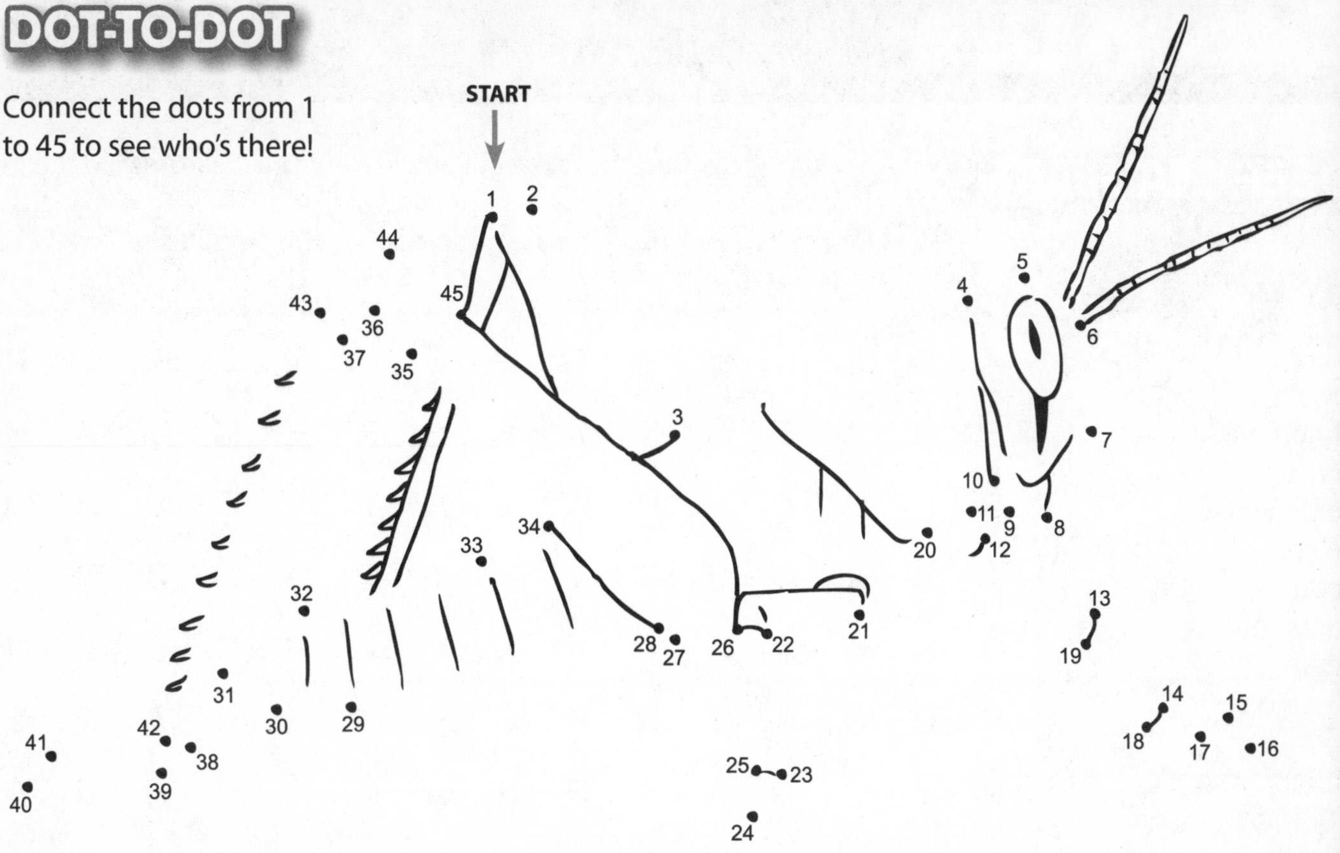

PICTURE THIS

Can you name the bugs spelled out in these rebuses?

1)

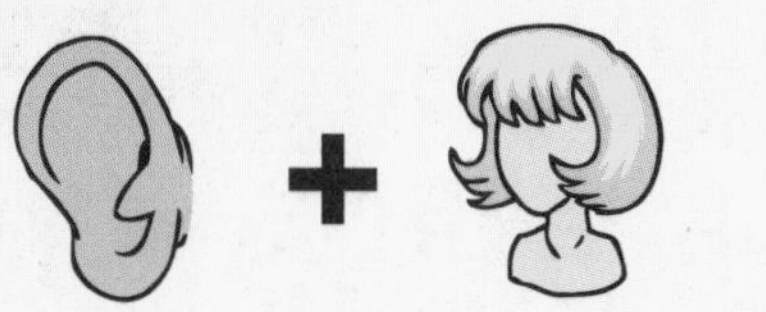

2)

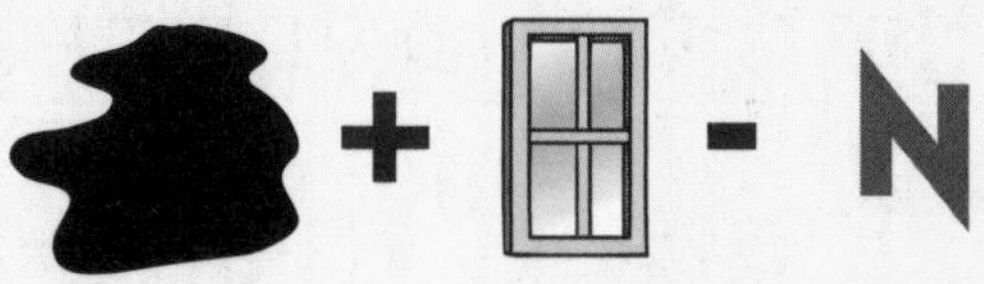

3)

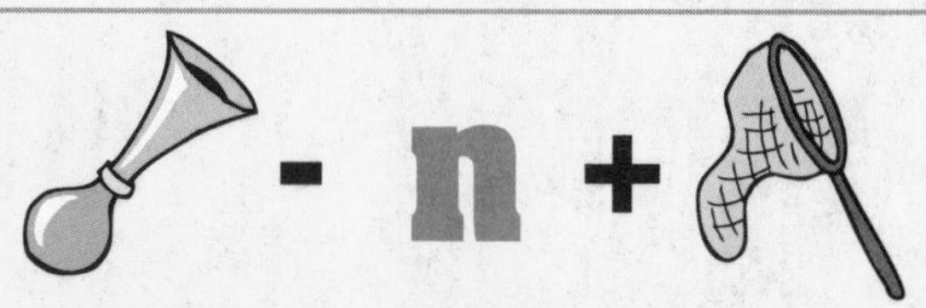

4)

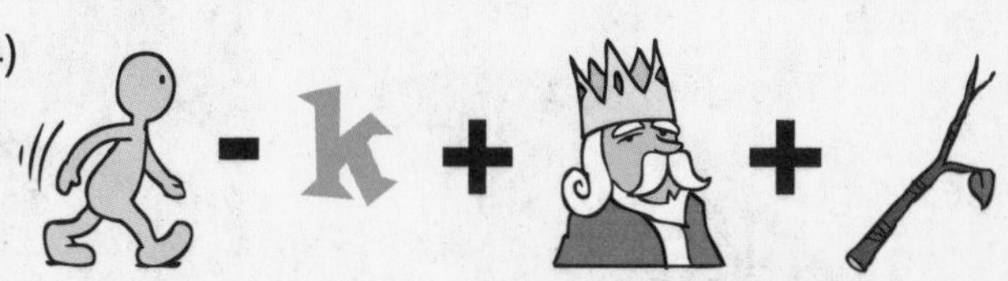

Ocean Life

DEEP-SEA SEARCH

See if you can find the names of 30 different sea creatures hidden in the puzzle below. Look across, up, down, diagonally, and backwards. Words in parentheses ( ) are not hidden in the puzzle.

anemone
barracuda
blue whale
clam
cod
devil ray
eel
flounder
grouper
hammerhead
jellyfish
lamprey
mackerel
man-o-war
octopus
orca
oyster
porpoise
puffer (fish)
sailfish
sea bass
sea turtle
seahorse
shark
shrimp
skate
snapper
squid
swordfish
tuna

A	B	L	Q	X	S	G	G	S	Y	T	D	W	G	P
E	D	Z	E	H	D	A	E	H	R	E	M	M	A	H
S	U	U	A	R	R	W	S	R	V	L	S	V	H	M
I	S	R	C	E	E	I	Z	I	C	A	W	S	R	A
O	K	A	T	A	F	K	L	M	L	H	O	E	E	N
P	C	S	B	Y	R	R	C	P	A	W	R	A	P	O
R	Y	O	L	A	A	R	B	A	M	E	D	H	U	W
O	H	L	D	Y	E	C	A	J	M	U	F	O	O	A
P	E	T	A	K	S	S	T	B	E	L	I	R	R	R
J	S	E	A	T	U	R	T	L	E	B	S	S	G	E
R	E	D	N	U	O	L	F	T	L	H	H	E	H	P
A	N	E	M	O	N	E	Y	E	R	P	M	A	L	P
V	D	L	S	U	P	O	T	C	O	O	R	C	A	A
Z	K	R	H	P	U	F	F	E	R	A	N	U	T	N
S	Q	U	I	D	S	A	I	L	F	I	S	H	K	S

FUN FACT:
The puffer fish can enlarge itself by filling with water. By doing so, it can discourage any enemies looking for an easy meal.

FISHBOWL BLUES

See if you can figure out which fish belongs in each bowl. The bowls are labeled with part of an exotic fish's name (for example, **LOW ANG** would be Yel**low** **Tang**). Use the list of fish on the left to help you out, although not all of them are used.

Purple Tang
Percula Clownfish
Royal Gramma
Rock Beauty
Yellow Tang
Clown Triggerfish
Volitan Lionfish
Flame Angelfish
Regal Tang
Queen Angelfish
Blue Damselfish
Regal Angelfish

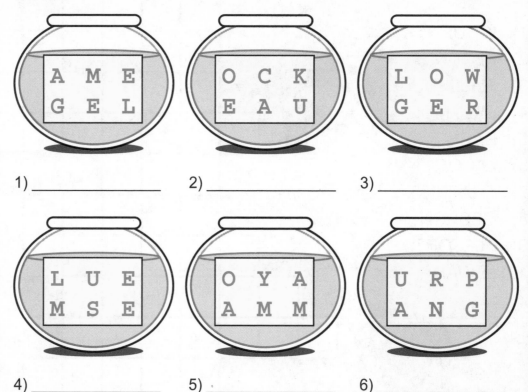

```
A M E        O C K        L O W
G E L        E A U        G E R
```

1) _____ 2) _____ 3) _____

```
L U E        O Y A        U R P
M S E        A M M        A N G
```

4) _____ 5) _____ 6) _____

CLOWNING AROUND

Help the clownfish get through the sea anemone.

START →

END

UNDERSEA SCRAMBLE

Unscramble the names of these undersea creatures and write your answers in the numbered rows going across. When you're done, read the green column of letters from top to bottom to reveal the name of a primitive fish once thought to be extinct.

1) ICHURN
2) PLODNIH
3) FLEJISHLY
4) SKULMOL
5) RACB
6) LACOR
7) SHAFRIST
8) GESPON
9) BLETORS
10) LEWAH

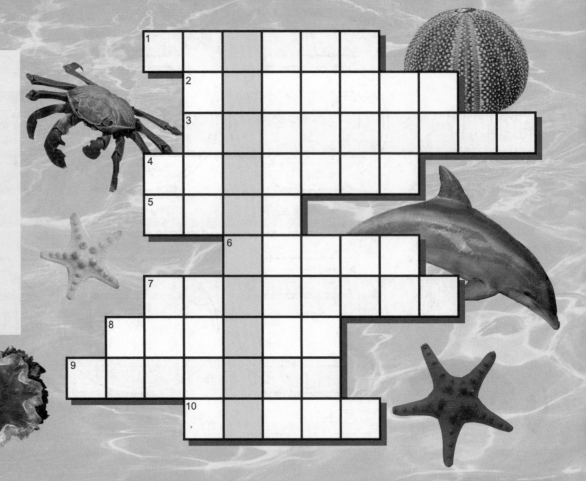

SHARK, SHARK!

This shark is all mixed up! See if you can put him back in order by labeling each piece with the numbers 1-6.

DOT-TO-DOT

Connect the dots to see who's there!

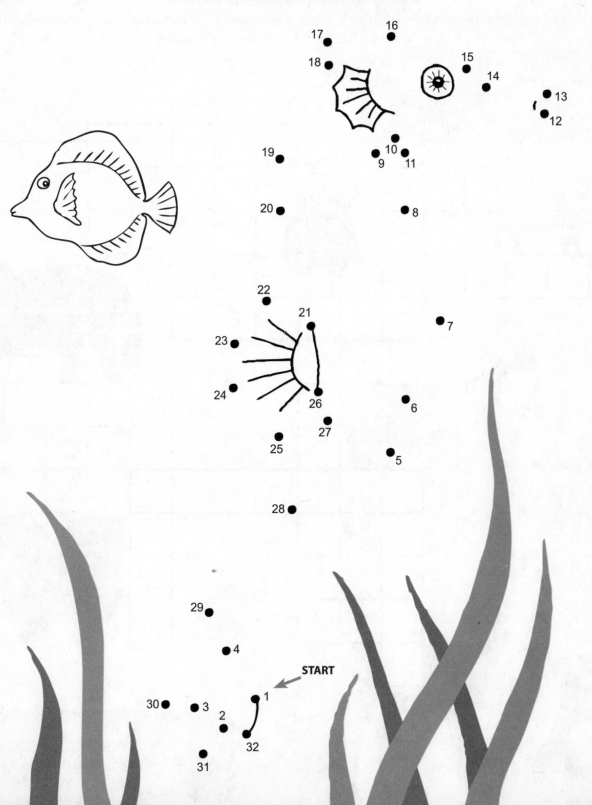

Barnyard Brainteasers

DOWN ON THE FARM

Can you identify each of the 14 farm animals pictured below and fit its name into the puzzle grid? The words can go across and down. We left an E-I-E-I-O to help you get started.

CHICKEN RIDDLE

Figure out the farm-related clues below, writing your answers in the spaces provided. Then use the numbered letters to fill in the puzzle grid and find the answer to the riddle!

A) The skin of a horse or cow

13	18	19	

B) Cows and bulls

		1	8		10

C) A male chicken

	7	11		6	14	

D) Sound a turkey makes

3	2			17	4

E) Area where animals graze

			12		15	20	

F) Chickens do this in the dirt

16					5		9

Why did the chicken cross the playground?

1	2		3	4	5		6	7		8	9	10
11	12	13	14	15			16	17	18	19	20	

JEEPERS PEEPERS

Can you draw 2 straight lines to round up these chicks into 4 equal groups?

Pet Puzzles

MAN'S BEST FRIEND

See if you can find the names of 30 different breeds of dog hidden in the puzzle below. Look across, up, down, diagonally, and backwards.

```
L B C O L L I E F F I T S A M Y
A D X C P E D N U O H Y E R G O
B A R N A I N A R E M O P U U R
R U B E U N R H L H B Y P Z B K
A H O A H A O E M M K E T U D S
D A X B S P E U L S A H A N G H
O U E L B S E S U I I T A G R I
R H R O U R E H E H E L I E L R
R I G O L E R T S G D W Z A O E
E H R D L K L K H N N U T P N T
T C E H D C V D U O A I C T Z E
R O A O O O I O O N U M K X O R
I R T U G C F C H O W N R E D R
E G D N T W U C B T P S D E P I
V I A D E O S H E E P D O G G E
E X N N F D A C H S H U N D T R
R R R E V E I R T E R N E D L O G
I S A I N T B E R N A R D C M B
```

basset hound
beagle
bloodhound
boxer
bulldog
chihuahua
chow
cocker spaniel
collie
corgi
dachshund
dalmatian
german shepherd
golden retriever
great dane
greyhound
husky
labrador retriever
mastiff
newfoundland
pekingese
pomeranian
poodle
pug
rottweiler
saint bernard
schnauzer
sheepdog
shih tzu
yorkshire terrier

CATS & DOGS

Help the cats and dogs work together to get through the maze below. You must follow an alternating path of dog, cat, dog, cat all the way from start to finish. You can move up and down and side to side, but not diagonally. Stay away from the animal warden!

START

FINISH

MORE PETS

Can you fit the names of the pictured pets into the rows going across? When you're done, read the blue column of letters from top to bottom to find the name of a very exotic pet.

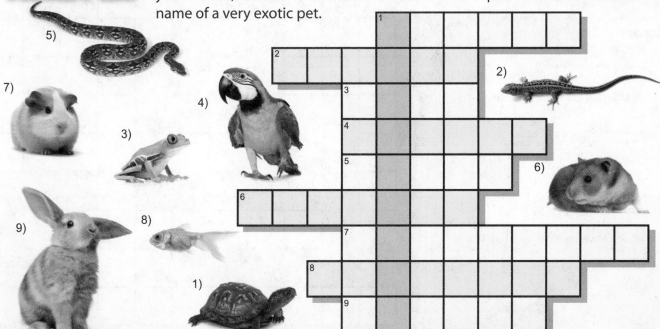

5)

7)

4)

3)

9)

8)

1)

35

Field and Forest

CRITTER CROSSWORD

How well do you know your woodland critters?
Fill in this crossword to find out!

Across:

1) buck-toothed dam builder

3) defends itself with foul odors

5) types of this animal include black and grizzly

6) types of this animal include timber and grey

7) has long ears and lives in a burrow

12) has red fur and a bushy tail

13) this bird is often called "wise"

14) looks like it is wearing a mask

15) like a squirrel, but is smaller and has stripes on its back

16) this bird uses its beak to pick bugs out from under the bark of trees

Down:

2) a large, deerlike animal

3) a good tree climber that loves nuts

4) a stag or doe

6) "Pop goes the _____"

8) short-legged, heavyset mammal that hunts by digging

9) this ferretlike mammal has a man's name

10) "How much wood can a _____ chuck?"

11) tiny rodent

DOT-TO-DOT

Connect the dots from 1 to 48.

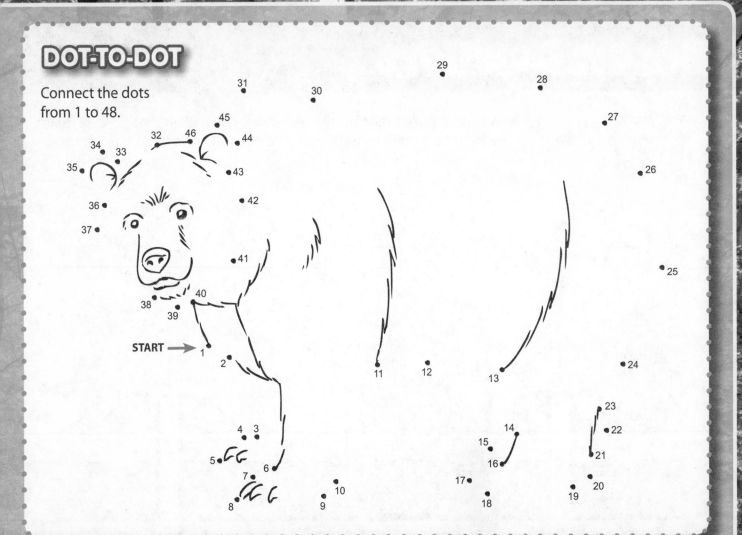

TOOTHY TWOSOME

Can you spot 2 beavers that look exactly alike?

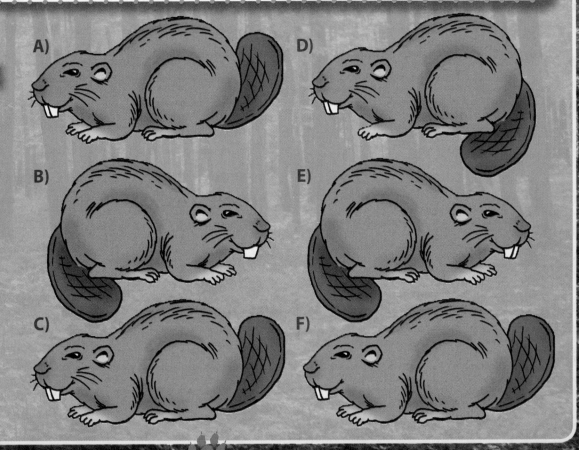

A)

B)

C)

D)

E)

F)

Desert Dwellers

HOME SWEET HOME

Prairie dogs build their burrows with more than one entrance in case they need to escape from a predator. Help these little guys test out their burrow.

START

END

PICTURE THIS

Can you name the desert animals spelled out in these rebuses?

1)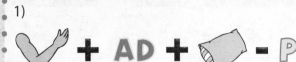

_____

2)

_____

3)

_____

4)

_____

SANDY SCRAMBLE

Unscramble the names of these desert animals and write your answers in the numbered rows going across. When you're done, read the blue column of letters from top to bottom to reveal the name of a tiny desert mammal that gets water from the seeds it eats.

1) KAWH
2) MELCA
3) ANGUIA
4) PHEGOR
5) GLEEA
6) LEVUURT
7) RINSCOOP
8) ROBRU
9) CIPPENRUO
10) VENAR
11) GNATMUS

Rainforest Follies

JUNGLE HUNT

See if you can find the names of 26 different rainforest creatures hidden in the puzzle below. Look across, up, down, diagonally, and backwards.

- basilisk lizard
- blue morpho
- caiman
- capybara
- chameleon
- chimpanzee
- civet
- gibbon
- hornbill
- howler monkey
- jaguar
- leafcutter ant
- lovebird
- macaw
- ocelot
- orangutan
- piranha
- puma
- quetzal
- sloth
- spider monkey
- tapir
- tarsier
- toucan
- tree frog
- vampire bat

```
C D R A Z I L K S I L I S A B
A R P U M A C A W O C O T L B
P R C S L O T H K C A L U L S
Y A N O B T O N C E I E O C P
B U R U O R U A F L M A R H I
A G Y A N E C R P O A F E I D
R A I B N E A I R T N C I M E
A J I B T F N P O M I U S P R
C L R E B R H M O N K T R A M
L K V L I O R A N G U T A N O
N I Z P Q G N T A P I E T Z N
C H A M E L E O N Q U R U E K
T T K T A B E R I P M A V E E
T O U H O W L E R M O N K E Y
V D R I B E V O L A Z T E U Q
```

FUN FACT:
Capybaras are the world's largest living rodents and excellent swimmers. They can even sleep in the water by keeping their noses just above the surface.

MONKEY BUSINESS

Figure out the jungle-themed clues below and write your answers in the spaces provided. Then use the numbered letters to fill in the puzzle grid and find the answer to the joke!

A) A type of small ape

7	5			16	10

D) One of the largest snakes in the world

		12	13			17	15	

B) A bird with a very large, colorful bill

3	2			9	1

E) The *blue morpho* is a type of _____

8		18	19				21	

C) A big black jungle cat

	20	6		4	

F) The *Burmese python* is a type of _____

14		11	22	

What did the banana say to the monkey?

1	2	3	4	5	6	7	–	8	9	10	11	12	13	14
■	15	16	17	'	18	■	19	20	21	22	!	■	■	

WORD WHEEL

Starting with the P marked by the purple arrow, move clockwise around the wheel, writing down every third letter on the spaces below. When you're done, the name of a highly toxic jungle animal will be revealed. The first 2 letters are done for you.

P O __ __ __ __ __

__ __ __ __

__ __ __ __

African Animals

SUDOKU ON SAFARI

Try to complete these puzzles by filling in the missing numbers. Each small empty box can be filled with a number from 1 to 9. However, each number can only be used once in each 3 x 3 grid. Also, each number can only be used once in each row across and down throughout the full puzzle.

Here is an example of what a finished puzzle looks like:

5	6	2	7	3	1	8	9	4
9	1	7	8	4	2	6	3	5
4	3	8	9	6	5	7	1	2
2	9	4	6	8	3	1	5	7
7	5	6	2	1	4	3	8	9
1	8	3	5	9	7	4	2	6
8	2	1	4	7	9	5	6	3
3	7	5	1	2	6	9	4	8
6	4	9	3	5	8	2	7	1

Puzzle 1:

	5			2	7			
8	4	2				5		6
7	6		4					3
	3			4			2	
5	7		2	3		6		8
			5	8		7	3	9
4					5			2
3	2	5		9			6	
		7	3			2		4

Puzzle 2:

		8		7				9
	2		1		5	3	6	
3		4		2				
	9			4				2
6	7	3	2		9		4	
4	5	2			8	7		
	4					2	8	3
2		7	4	5		9		
		6			1		7	

FUN FACT:
The giraffe's patterned fur helps hide it from predators.

SAVANNAH SCRAMBLE

Unscramble the names of each of these animals from Africa and write your answers in the rows going across. When you're done, read the blue column of letters from top to bottom to discover the biggest land animal of them all.

1) BRAZE
2) KAAJCL
3) TERMAEK
4) PENTOLEA
5) NAYEH
6) FIRAGEF
7) ONIL
8) CHOSTRI

DOT-TO-DOT

Connect the dots from 1 to 61 to see who's there!

Polar Puzzles

COOL CRITTERS

There are many animals that live and thrive in freezing cold temperatures. See if you can fit the list of Arctic and Antarctic animals below into the puzzle. There's a north P-O-L-E and a south P-O-L-E to help you get started.

ARCTIC FOX
ARCTIC TERN
BELUGA (whale)
CARIBOU
ERMINE
HARP SEAL
MUSK OX
NARWHAL

PENGUIN
POLAR BEAR
PTARMIGAN
SNOWY OWL
TUNDRA WOLF
WALRUS
WOLVERINE

After you're done, unscramble the orange circled letters to spell the name of one of the penguin's deadliest predators.

A MOTHER'S JOURNEY

Help this mother polar bear get back to her cub.

START →

END ↓

A PECK OF PENGUINS

Did you know that there are at least 17 different types of penguin? See if you can find them all in this puzzle. Look across, up, down, diagonally, and backwards.

adélie	macaroni
african	magellanic
black-footed	rockhopper
chinstrap	royal
emperor	snares
erect-crested	yellow-eyed
fiordland	
gentoo	
humboldt	
king	
little blue	

```
D C H I N S T R A P Z X
E E I U N A F R I C A N
Y O T N M O K I N G D L
E X O S A B R G U Z E I
W M W T E L O A X U L T
O M P B N R L L C J I T
L Q N E K E C E D A E L
L A Y O R E G T G T M E
E D E T O O F K C A L B
Y V M S N A R E S E M L
F R O C K H O P P E R U
F I O R D L A N D V V E
```

Wonders Down Under

See if you can find the names of 30 animals from Australia and New Zealand hidden in the puzzle below. Look across, up, down, diagonally, and backwards. Words in parentheses ( ) are not hidden in the puzzle.

bandicoot
bilby
cassowary
cockatoo
crocodile
dingo
echidna
emu
frilled lizard
galah
kangaroo
kiwi
koala
kookaburra
kowari
magpie
monitor
platypus
(pygmy) possum
potaroo
quokka
quoll
(rainbow) lorikeet
sawfish
seadragon
sugar glider
tasmanian devil
thorny devil
wallaby
wombat

B D A S U P Y T A L P U U M E
A I A R R U B A K O O K M C R
N N L O R I K E E T T A U R E
D G L B N O G A R D A E S O D
I O I A Y N K O W A R I S C I
C A S S O W A R Y S O S O O L
O Y O L K A N G A R O O P D G
O B L I V E D Y N R O H T I R
T A S M A N I A N D E V I L A
A L A O K L H U M A G P I E G
B L Q U L A C O C K A T O O U
M A B O L T E A K K O U Q P S
O W U A S R O T I N O M O G C
W Q G R H S I F W A S Y I P E
F R I L L E D L I Z A R D M T

FUN FACT:
Tasmanian Devils can only be found on the Australian island of Tasmania. They are *marsupials*, which means that their young are grown and raised in a pouch on the mother's belly.

DOT-TO-DOT

Connect the dots from 1 to 45 to see who's there!

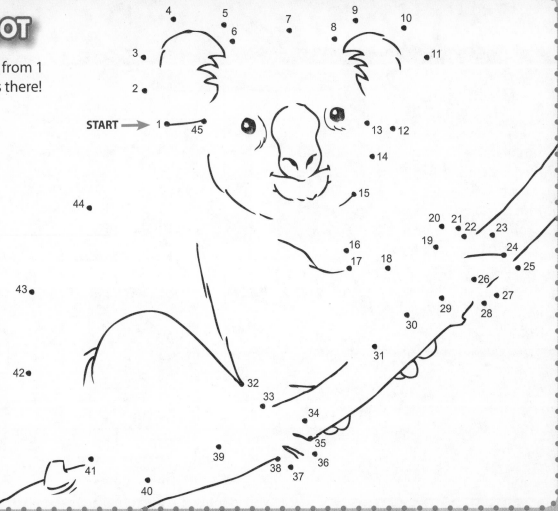

START

MIXED-UP MONITOR

This monitor lizard has gone to pieces. See if you can put him back in order by labeling each piece with the numbers 1-6.

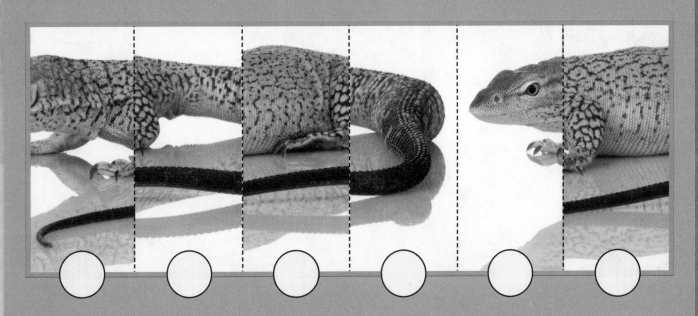

NIGHT LIFE

Animals that are more active at night than during the day are called **nocturnal**. Using the word NOCTURNAL as a starting point, see if you can fit the names from the word list into the puzzle grid. Words can go across and down.

AYE-AYE   BAT
CRICKET   RACCOON
MOTH   SKUNK
FROG   JERBOA
TOAD   TARSIER
PANGOLIN   OWL
OPOSSUM

N O C T U R N A L

CRITTER CLOSE-UPS

Can you identify the nocturnal animal seen in each of the pictures below?

1) _____

2) _____

3) _____

4) _____

5) _____

6) _____

7) _____

8) _____

9) _____

10) _____

CATCHING FIREFLIES

You need a friend to play this game. Each player takes a turn connecting 2 neighboring dots with a straight line. You can go up and down and side to side, but not diagonally. Try to be the player who makes a box by adding the last line of a square. When you do, write your initial in the box and take an extra turn. Each plain square is worth 1 point; a square with a firefly in it is worth 2 points. The player with the highest score wins!

Game 1   Score_____   _____

Game 2   Score_____   _____

Answers

Page 4: Creature Combos

ant + lion
bull + frog
cat + fish
chicken + hawk
deer + tick
horse + fly

kangaroo + rat
fox + hound
stag + beetle
tiger + shark
wolf + spider

Page 5: Beastly Babies

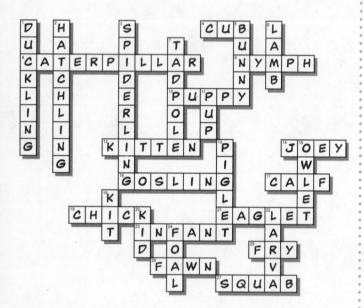

Page 6: Animal Scramble

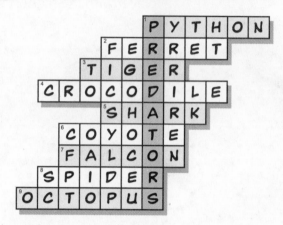

Page 7: Group Troop

1) school
2) family
3) cackle
4) herd

5) stand
6) pack
7) pride
8) swarm

9) gaggle
10) bed
11) cloud
12) murder

Page 8: Critter Close-Ups

1) rabbit
2) bee
3) gorilla
4) parrot
5) pig

6) caterpillar
7) crocodile
8) armadillo
9) shark
10) tiger

Page 6: Talk Like the Animals

BEE - BUZZ
BIRD - CHIRP
CAT - MEOW
CHICKEN - CLUCK
COW - MOO
CROW - CAW
DOG - BARK
DONKEY - HEEHAW
DUCK - QUACK
FROG - RIBBIT
GOOSE - HONK
HORSE - NEIGH
LION - ROAR
MOUSE - SQUEAK
OWL - HOOT
PARROT - SQUAWK
PIG - OINK
SHEEP - BAA
SNAKE - HISS
TURKEY - GOBBLE

Secret Sound:

COCK-A-DOODLE-DOO (rooster)

Page 8: Simile Safari

1) bat
2) fox
3) dog
4) lamb
5) mule
6) bee

7) mouse
8) ox
9) eel
10) clam
11) bird
12) peacock

Page 10: Mammal Mania Word Search

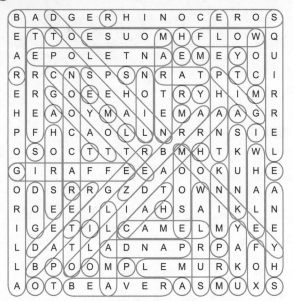

THE MYSTERY MAMMAL IS THE HIPPOPOTAMUS

Page 11: Big Kitty Crossword

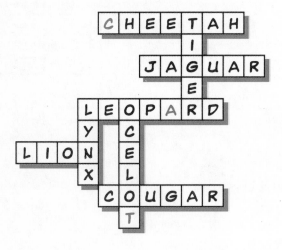

Page 12: Mammal Scramble

LEMUR   SLOTH   RABBIT   MONKEY

Q: Which side of a gorilla has the most hair?
A: THE OUTSIDE

Page 12: Picture This

1) ant + eat + er = ANTEATER
2) baby - y + moon - m = BABOON
3) man + a + tee = MANATEE
4) orange -e + u + tank - k = ORANGUTAN

Page 14: Reptile Roundup

Page 16: Serpent Search

THE FEAR OF SNAKES IS CALLED OPHIDIOPHOBIA

Page 17: A Slithery Saying

RED ON BLACK - WON'T ATTACK;
RED ON YELLOW - DEADLY FELLOW

The snake shown is venomous.

Page 18: Salamander

Here are 105 words made from the letters in SALAMANDER. Can you think of any more?

a	drama	mane	ream
alas	dramas	manes	reams
alma	dream	mare	red
alms	dreams	mares	reds
amen	ear	Mars	remand
amend	earn	mead	rend
amends	earns	mean	rends
an	ears	means	salad
and	end	medal	sale
are	ends	medals	same
area	lad	men	same
areas	laden	mend	sand
arm	lads	mends	sandal
armada	lam	name	sander
armadas	lame	named	sane
armed	land	names	seal
arms	lands	near	seam
as	lard	nears	sear
dam	lead	nerd	send
dame	leads	nerds	slam
dams	learn	ram	slander
damsel	lend	rams	sled
dare	lends	ran	smear
dares	made	read	snare
deal	male	reads	
deals	males	realm	
dear	man	realms	

Page 19: Frogs & Toads

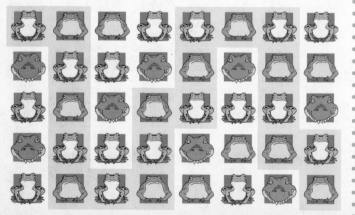

Page 19: A Number of Newts

D and F are the same

Page 20: Sky-High Sudoku

5	2	8	9	4	6	7	3	1
7	3	9	5	1	2	8	4	6
6	1	4	7	8	3	9	2	5
3	9	1	4	5	8	2	6	7
2	5	6	3	7	9	1	8	4
4	8	7	6	2	1	3	5	9
1	7	2	8	6	4	5	9	3
9	4	5	2	3	7	6	1	8
8	6	3	1	9	5	4	7	2

1	4	9	7	2	6	3	8	5
6	2	5	3	1	8	9	4	7
7	3	8	4	9	5	1	6	2
5	6	3	1	4	7	8	2	9
9	8	4	2	5	3	7	1	6
2	1	7	8	6	9	5	3	4
3	9	1	6	7	2	4	5	8
4	5	2	9	8	1	6	7	3
8	7	6	5	3	4	2	9	1

Page 21: Hummingbird Humor

A) DOWN   E) YELLOW
B) ROBIN   F) DUCK
C) NECTAR   G) NEST
D) WHO   H) FEATHERS

Q: Why do hummingbirds hum?
A: BECAUSE THEY DON'T KNOW THE WORDS.

Page 21: A Pair of Lovebirds

C and E are the same

Page 22: Feathered Fugitives

1) Mourning Dove   4) Yellow Warbler
2) Pigmy Nuthatch   5) Barn Swallow
3) American Robin   6) Mountain Chickadee

Page 22: Picture This

1) road + runner = ROADRUNNER
2) king + fish + er = KINGFISHER
3) sand + pipe + er = SANDPIPER
4) magnet - net + pie = MAGPIE

Page 23: Bird Search

Page 24: Bugs, Bugs, Bugs!

Page 25: Creepy Crawly Crossword

Page 27: Picture This

1) ear + wig = EARWIG
2) black + window - n = BLACK WIDOW
3) horn - n + net = HORNET
4) walk - k + king + stick = WALKING STICK

Page 28: Deep-Sea Search

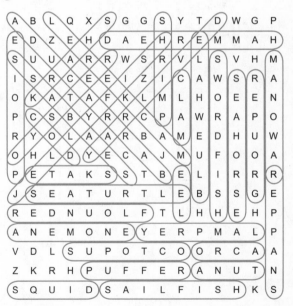

Page 29: Fishbowl Blues

1) Flame Angelfish
2) Rock Beauty
3) Clown Triggerfish
4) Blue Damselfish
5) Royal Gramma
6) Purple Tang

Page 30: Undersea Scramble

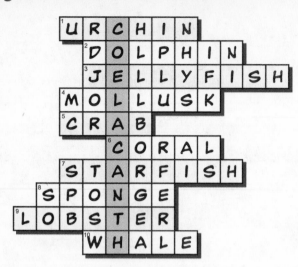

Page 30: Shark, Shark!

From left to right, the pictures are: 5-3-1-6-2-4

Page 32: Down on the Farm

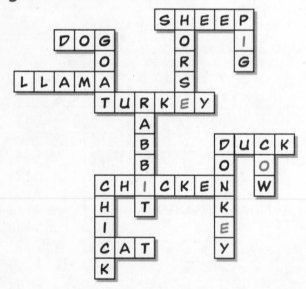

Page 33: Chicken Riddle

A) HIDE   D) GOBBLE
B) CATTLE   E) PASTURE
C) ROOSTER   F) SCRATCH

Q: Why did the chicken cross the playground?
A: TO GET TO THE OTHER SLIDE.

Page 33: Jeepers Peepers

Page 34: Man's Best Friend

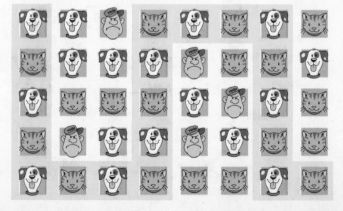

Page 35: Cats & Dogs

Page 35: More Pets

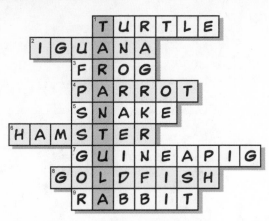

TURTLE
IGUANA
FROG
PARROT
SNAKE
HAMSTER
GUINEAPIG
GOLDFISH
RABBIT

Page 36: Critter Crossword

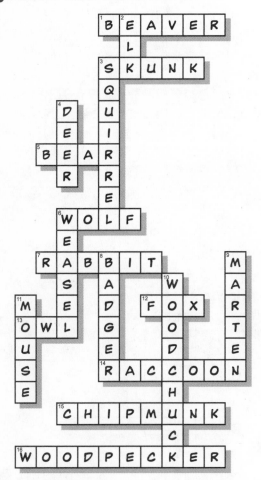

BEAVER
SKUNK
DEER
BEAR
WOLF
RABBIT
MARTEN
MOUSE
OWL
FOX
WOODCHUCK
RACCOON
CHIPMUNK
WOODPECKER

Page 37: Toothy Twosome

A and C are the same

Page 39: Picture This

1) arm + ad + pillow − pw = ARMADILLO
2) jack + crab − c − bite − e = JACKRABBIT
3) rattle + sn + cake − c = RATTLESNAKE
4) star − s + ant + hula − h = TARANTULA

Page 39: Sandy Scramble

HAWK
CAMEL
IGUANA
GOPHER
EAGLE
VULTURE
SCORPION
BURRO
★
PORCUPINE
RAVEN
MUSTANG

Page 40: Jungle Hunt

Page 41: Monkey Business

A) GIBBON
B) TOUCAN
C) PANTHER
D) ANACONDA
E) BUTTERFLY
F) SNAKE

Q: What did the banana say to the monkey?
A: NOTHING – BANANAS DON'T TALK!

Page 41: Word Wheel

POISON DART FROG

Page 42: Sudoku On Safari

9	5	3	6	2	7	4	8	1
8	4	2	9	1	3	5	7	6
7	6	1	4	5	8	2	9	3
6	3	8	7	4	9	1	2	5
5	7	9	2	3	1	6	4	8
2	1	4	5	8	6	7	3	9
4	9	6	8	7	5	3	1	2
3	2	5	1	9	4	8	6	7
1	8	7	3	6	2	9	5	4

5	6	8	3	7	4	1	2	9
7	2	9	1	8	5	3	6	4
3	1	4	9	6	2	8	5	7
8	9	1	5	4	7	6	3	2
6	7	3	2	1	9	5	4	8
4	5	2	6	3	8	7	9	1
1	4	5	7	9	6	2	8	3
2	8	7	4	5	3	9	1	6
9	3	6	8	2	1	4	7	5

Page 43: Savannah Scramble

1) ZEBRA
2) JACKAL
3) MEERKAT
4) ANTELOPE
5) HYENA
6) GIRAFFE
7) LION
8) OSTRICH

Biggest land mammal: ELEPHANT

Page 44: Cool Critters

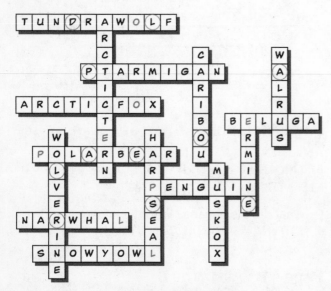

Penguin predator:
LEOPARD
SEAL

Page 45: A Peck of Penguins

Page 46: Wonders Down Under

Page 47: Mixed-Up Monitor

From left to right, the pictures are: 2-5-4-6-1-3

Page 48: Night Life

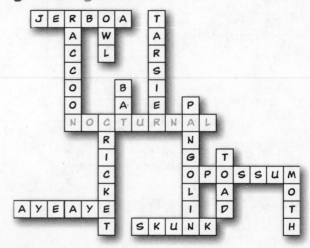

Page 48: Critter Close-Ups

1) skunk
2) owl
3) cricket
4) opossum
5) bat
6) frog
7) hedgehog
8) moth
9) raccoon
10) catfish